To Mom and Aunt Cheryl,
two amazing, strong women that taught me
the importance of sharing my voice. Katie Parker

For my beautiful girls, Ainsley and Sage. Aubrey Stout

Each day of life I know I have a choice.

you still can hear my voice.

I'll sing out strong! I'll share my light!
I'll share my voice, with others every day.

I'll make the choice, to stand for right along the way.

And as I grow, my voice will become strong.

I'll share my voice

come sing along!

And as I grow, my voice will become strong.

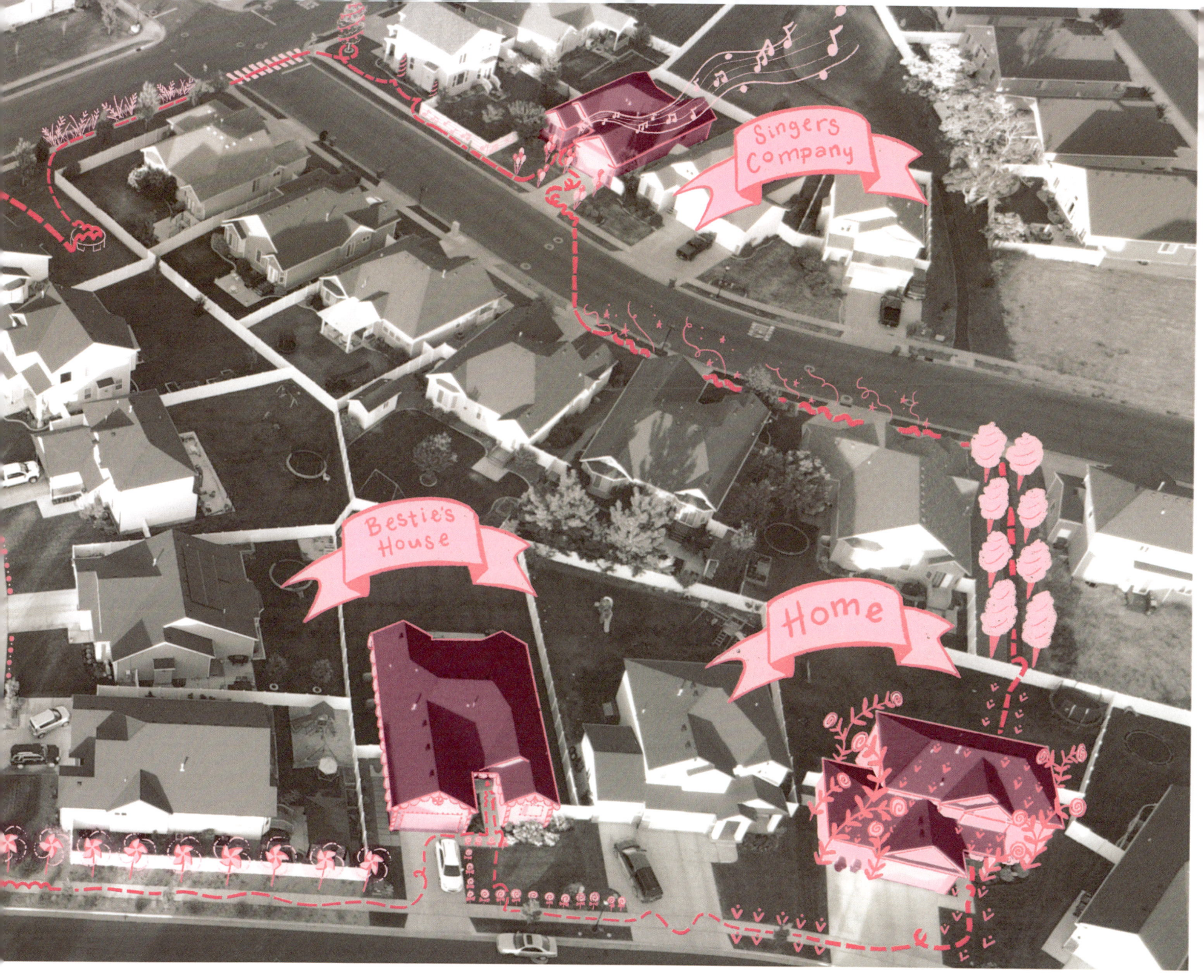

I'll share my voice,

Dear Girls,

I hope you always remember this world needs YOUR light and goodness through your voice every day. You are wonderful, good and strong! Be brave, be bold and build! You are the future and it is BRIGHT!

Love,
Miss Katie

On-line you can find more about what we do to inspire young girls to grow! Ask for your parent's help to check out: Bloomfully.com "A Place Where Girls Grow" and home of Singers Company & I Believe in Me.

Singers Company is an award-winning franchise opportunity for amazing women. We are always looking for strong women with big hearts and a desire to strengthen young girls and make a positive impact on their own lives, families and communities. Check out singerscompany.com for more information.

Singers Company, Provo, Utah 84604

Copyright 2024 by Bloomfully, LLC. DBA Singers Company.

All rights reserved, including the right of reproduction in whole or in part in any form. Book design by Aubrey and Nathan Stout. Written and manufactured in the USA and by contract available worldwide.

No portion of this book may be reproduced in any form without written permission from the publisher or author, except as permitted by U.S. copyright law.

Color interior illustrations and exterior artwork completed by Aubrey Stout. Original song lyrics by Katie Parker.

Parker, Katie.

I'll share my voice.

Milton Keynes UK
Ingram Content Group UK Ltd.
UKRC031412091224
452083UK00002B/3